AF867310

The Insurance Survival Guide: What's Covered and What Isn't

Copyright © 2026 by Andrew DeCarlo.

ISBN (eBook/Kindle): 979-8-9970236-0-7

ISBN (Paperback): 979-8-9970236-1-4

ISBN (Hardcover): 979-8-9970236-2-1

Library Of Congress Catalog Card Number: Applied.

All rights reserved. No part of this book may be reproduced or transmitted in any form or by any means, electronic or mechanical, including photocopying, recording, or by any information storage and retrieval system without express written permission from the author, except in the case of brief quotations embodied in critical reviews and certain other noncommercial uses permitted by copyright law.

Published in the United States of America by Lynx Publishers.

The Insurance Survival Guide: What's Covered and What Isn't

ANDREW DECARLO

LYNX
PUBLISHERS

Dear friend,

Before you go any further, I want to tell you something that almost no insurance book, agent, brochure, or website will ever say out loud:

What you don't get matters more than what you do.

Every policy looks reassuring on the surface. Every plan sounds complete. Every brochure is designed to make you feel protected. But buried underneath the comforting language and the polished promises is the part that actually determines your future the exclusions, the limitations, the exceptions, the loopholes the things you thought were covered but aren't.

This book is not here to sell you anything.

It's not here to make insurance look pretty. It's not here to repeat the same generic explanations you've already heard. This book exists for one reason: to expose what's missing. Because that's where people get hurt. That's where the surprises happen. That's where the bills come from. That's where the heartbreak starts. You deserve to know the truth the full truth not just the convenient parts. So on every page, you'll see two things side by side:

1. *What your insurance does cover*
2. *What your insurance absolutely does NOT cover!*

No sugarcoating. No softening. No hiding the fine print in the shadows.

If you've ever felt confused, misled, or blindsided by insurance, this book will finally give you the clarity you've been missing. Not because of what's included... but because of what's not.

Let's begin. The truth is waiting.

Author
Andrew De Carlo

Table of Contents

Health Insurance

Health insurance generally covers four big buckets of medical care doctor visits, hospital care, prescription drugs, and surgeries but each plan defines the details differently. The Affordable Care Act requires all Marketplace plans to cover a core set of Essential Health Benefits, which include these categories.

Medical Care routine & specialist visits

Health insurance covers most types of outpatient medical care, usually with a copay or coinsurance after you meet your deductible.

- Primary care visits checkups, sick visits, chronic condition management.
- Specialists cardiology, dermatology, endocrinology, orthopedics, etc.
- Preventive care vaccines, annual physicals, screenings (mammograms, colonoscopies). Preventive services are usually free under ACA rules.
- Diagnostic tests bloodwork, X-rays, ultrasounds, MRIs.
- Mental health care therapy, psychiatry, substance-use treatment (required under ACA).

Hospital Visits emergency & inpatient care

Hospital care is one of the most expensive categories, and insurance covers:

- Emergency room visits
- Urgent care
- Inpatient hospitalization room/board, nursing care, medications, tests
- ICU care
- Outpatient hospital procedures same-day surgeries, imaging, infusions

Plans differ in how they charge:

- Some use a flat copay for ER visits.
- Others apply deductible + coinsurance (e.g., 20% of the bill).
- Staying "in-network" is critical out-of-network hospital care can be dramatically more expensive.

Prescription Drugs medications

All ACA-compliant plans must cover prescription medications, but each plan has a formulary (a list of covered drugs) organized into tiers:

- Tier 1: generics (lowest cost)
- Tier 2: preferred brand-name
- Tier 3: non-preferred brand
- Tier 4/5: specialty drugs (highest cost)

Plans may require:

- Prior authorization
- Step therapy (try cheaper drugs first)
- Quantity limits

Marketplace guidance emphasizes checking your plan's drug list to confirm coverage.

Surgeries inpatient & outpatient

Health insurance covers medically necessary surgeries, including:

- Emergency surgeries appendectomy, trauma surgery
- Elective but medically necessary surgeries hernia repair, gallbladder removal
- Orthopedic surgeries knee/hip replacements
- Cardiac surgeries bypass, valve repair
- Cancer-related surgeries tumor removal, mastectomy

Coverage usually includes:

- Surgeon fees
- Anesthesiology
- Operating room costs
- Post-operative care
- Follow-up visits

Cosmetic surgeries (e.g., facelifts, liposuction) are not covered, unless medically necessary (e.g., breast reconstruction after mastectomy).

How costs work across all categories

Every plan uses the same basic cost-sharing structure:

- Premium — monthly cost to keep the plan active
- Deductible what you pay before insurance starts sharing costs
- Copay fixed amount (e.g., $25 per visit)
- Coinsurance percentage of the bill (e.g., 20%)
- Out-of-pocket maximum once you hit this, insurance pays 100% for the rest of the year

Other major categories health insurance covers

Each of these is also an ACA Essential Health Benefit:

- Maternity & newborn care
- Rehabilitation & physical therapy
- Laboratory services
- Pediatric care
- Mental health & substance-use treatment
- Preventive & wellness services

Life Insurance

The Two Big Categories of Life Insurance

The entire life insurance world boils down to term life and whole life. Everything else universal life, variable life, indexed life is just a complicated remix of whole life.

Term Life Insurance

Simple, Cheap, and Usually the Right Choice

What it is:

Term life is pure insurance. You pay for a set number of years (10, 20, 30). If you die during that term, your family gets the money. If you outlive the term, the policy ends.

What you're buying:

Protection, not an investment.

Why people like it:

- Low cost for a large amount of coverage
- Straightforward no cash value, no games
- Perfect for working families who need protection while kids are growing up or a mortgage is being paid

Why insurance agents don't like selling it:

They earn tiny commissions compared to whole life.

Who term life is for:

- People who want the most coverage for the lowest price
- People who don't want to mix insurance with investing
- People who want something simple and honest

What to avoid:

- "Return of premium" term overpriced
- Term that automatically converts to whole life without you noticing.

Whole Life Insurance

Expensive, Complex, and Often Oversold

What it is:

Whole life lasts your entire life and includes a savings account called cash value. Part of your premium goes toward insurance, and part goes into this cash value.

What you're buying:

A combination of insurance + a forced savings plan.

Why it's controversial:

- Very expensive often 10–20× the cost of term
- Cash value grows slowly
- Hard to understand
- Agents push it because commissions are huge

Who whole life is actually appropriate for:

- High-income individuals who have already maxed out retirement accounts
- People with complex estate planning needs
- People who need lifelong coverage for a dependent with special needs

Who it is not for:

- The average family
- Anyone who is being pressured into it
- Anyone who hasn't already built an emergency fund and retirement savings

Red flags:

- "This is an investment."
- "This policy pays for itself."
- "You can borrow from it anytime."
- "You'll never lose money."

These are sales lines, not financial truths.

The Simple Rule Most People Should Follow

For 99% of households, the most financially responsible choice is:

Buy inexpensive term life. Invest the difference elsewhere.

This keeps insurance as insurance and investing as investing.

How Much Coverage Should a Person Get?

- 10–15× annual income
- Enough to pay off the mortgage
- Enough to raise children to adulthood

This is not personalized financial advice just a common guideline used by many planners.

What People Should Watch Out For

Here are the traps that cause people to overpay:

- High-pressure sales
- Policies with confusing riders
- Mixing insurance with investing
- Policies pitched as "tax shelters"
- Policies sold to elderly people who don't need them

You can speak strongly here because you've lived it you've seen how the industry pushes products people don't need.

A Clean Summary

Term life is simple and affordable. Whole life is complex and expensive.

Most families only need term life. Whole life is for very specific, high-income situations — not the average household.

If you understand this one distinction, you'll avoid 90% of the mistakes people make with life insurance.

General Liability Insurance

General liability insurance in the United States is the core protection most business owners rely on to shield themselves from the most common and most expensive third-party claims. At its heart, general liability insurance (GLI) protects your business from lawsuits involving bodily injury, property damage, and advertising/personal injury that arise from normal operations.

What General Liability Insurance Covers (U.S. Business Owners)

- Bodily injury If a customer slips, falls, or is otherwise injured on your premises, GLI can cover medical bills, legal fees, and settlements.
- Property damage If your business accidentally damages someone else's property (e.g., contractor breaks a client's countertop), GLI pays for repair or replacement.
- Personal & advertising injury Covers claims of libel, slander, copyright infringement, or misleading advertising.
- Medical payments Pays for minor injuries to guests regardless of fault.
- Products & completed operations If your product or completed work causes injury or damage, GLI may cover resulting claims.
- Damage to premises rented to you Covers accidental fire or damage to a rented commercial space.

What General Liability Does Not Cover

- Professional mistakes → requires professional liability insurance.
- Employee injuries → requires workers' compensation.
- Damage to your own business property → requires commercial property insurance or a BOP.
- Intentional acts or fraud.
- Auto accidents involving business vehicles → requires commercial auto insurance.

Typical Cost for U.S. Business Owners

Costs vary by industry, size, and risk level, but national data shows:

- Median cost: ~$55/month
- Average cost: ~$79/month

Higher-risk industries (construction, landscaping, contractors) pay more; low-risk service businesses pay less.

Why U.S. Business Owners Need GLI

- Protects against lawsuits that can easily reach five or six figures.
- Often required by landlords, clients, and contracts.
- Builds trust with customers and partners.
- Covers common everyday risks slips, falls, accidental damage, advertising disputes.

You can think of general liability insurance (GLI) limits as the financial shield size your business needs. The right limit depends on your industry risk, customer interaction level, contract requirements, and Florida-specific exposure. I'll walk you through a clear, step-by-step way to choose your limits so you feel confident you're not under-insured or overpaying.

The Short Answer

Most U.S. small businesses choose $1 million per occurrence / $2 million aggregate, but many Florida businesses especially those with customer foot traffic or contract work benefit from $2M/$4M or an umbrella policy for extra protection.

Identify Your Risk Category

Start by placing your business in one of these buckets:

- Low-risk service consultants, writers, online services, tutors
- Moderate-risk retail or office shops, salons, real estate offices
- High-risk trades contractors, landscapers, cleaning companies
- Very high-risk public exposure gyms, event venues, restaurants

Your category determines your baseline limit.

Match Risk Level to Recommended Limits

Risk Level	Typical GLI Limit	Why
Low-risk	$1M / $2M	Minimal physical interaction with customers
Moderate-risk	$1M / $2M or $2M / $4M	Foot traffic increases slip-and-fall exposure
High-risk	$2M / $4M + umbrella	Property damage & injury claims more likely
Very high-risk	$2M / $4M + $1M–$5M umbrella	High volume of customers, higher lawsuit risk

Check Contract Requirements

Look at:

- Landlord leases
- Vendor agreements
- Client contracts
- Government or municipal work requirements

Common contract requirements:

- $1M per occurrence
- $2M aggregate
- Additional insured endorsement
- Waiver of subrogation

If any contract requires higher limits, that becomes your minimum.

Estimate Your Worst-Case Scenario

Ask yourself:

- Could a customer be seriously injured on your premises?
- Could your work damage a client's expensive property?
- Could a lawsuit exceed $1M?

If the answer is "yes," you likely need $2M/$4M or an umbrella policy.

Decide Whether You Need an Umbrella Policy

Umbrella coverage adds $1M–$10M on top of your GLI limits.

You should consider an umbrella if:

- You work in clients' homes
- You have high customer foot traffic
- You operate in a litigious state (Florida qualifies)
- You want protection from rare but catastrophic claims

Putting It All Together A Simple Formula

Use this quick rule:

Your GLI limit should cover the most expensive accident your business could realistically cause.

Key Person Insurance

Key person insurance is one of the most strategic forms of business protection because it insures the people who make the business work, not the equipment or the building. Here's a clean, structured explanation.

What Key Person Insurance Is

Key person insurance is a life or disability policy a business buys on an essential employee whose loss would financially damage the company.

The business is:

- the owner of the policy
- the payer of the premiums
- the beneficiary of the payout

It's designed to keep the company alive if a crucial person dies or becomes disabled.

Who Counts as a "Key Person"

A key person is anyone whose absence would cause major financial disruption. Examples include:

- Founders the vision, relationships, and strategy live with them
- Top sales producers losing them means losing revenue
- Specialized experts engineers, scientists, designers
- Executives CFO, COO, or anyone who runs core operations
- Public-facing figures individuals whose reputation drives business

If the business would struggle to function without them, they're a key person.

What Key Person Insurance Covers

The payout helps the company:

- Replace lost revenue caused by the person's absence
- Hire and train a replacement
- Reassure lenders and investors
- Pay off debts if the business must downsize
- Buy out the deceased partner's shares (when paired with a buy-sell

agreement)

It's financial breathing room during a crisis.

Types of Key Person Insurance

- Key person life insurance pays if the key person dies
- Key person disability insurance pays if they become disabled and can't work
- Key person replacement insurance specifically covers recruitment and training costs

Most companies carry both life and disability because disability is statistically more likely.

How Much Coverage a Business Needs

Businesses usually calculate coverage based on:

- Revenue contribution (e.g., 5× the person's annual profit impact)
- Replacement cost (recruiting + training + lost productivity)
- Debt obligations tied to that person
- Investor or lender requirements

There's no universal formula, but the goal is to keep the company stable for 12–24 months.

Tax Treatment (U.S.)

- Premiums are not tax-deductible
- Payouts are generally tax-free

The business must follow IRS "notice and consent" rules

This keeps the policy classified as legitimate business protection rather than a tax shelter.

Why Key Person Insurance Matters

Think of it as business continuity insurance for human capital.

Companies don't fail because a building burns down they fail because the person who knows how everything works is suddenly gone.

Pet Insurance

What Pet Insurance Covers

Most accident-and-illness plans reimburse you for unexpected veterinary costs. You pay the vet, submit a claim, and get reimbursed.

- Accidents broken bones, bite wounds, swallowed objects, poisoning. Covered by all major insurers. Paws and Appeal...
- Illnesses infections, digestive issues, diabetes, arthritis, cancer. Standard in accident-and-illness plans.
- Emergency care ER visits, overnight hospitalization, surgery.
- Diagnostics X-rays, ultrasounds, bloodwork.
- Specialists oncologists, dermatologists, cardiologists. Many insurers allow any licensed U.S. vet.
- Optional wellness add-ons vaccines, dental cleanings, flea/tick prevention. Not included unless you buy a wellness rider.

What Pet Insurance Does NOT Cover (Common Exclusions)

- Pre-existing conditions anything your pet had symptoms of before enrollment. The #1 reason for claim denials. ...
- Routine care without a wellness plan vaccines, grooming, nail trims, dental cleanings.
- Breeding, pregnancy, or whelping almost always excluded.
- Cosmetic or elective procedures ear cropping, tail docking, declawing.
- Behavioral training unless a plan specifically includes it.
- Waiting period issues illnesses or injuries occurring before the waiting period ends. Example: MetLife has no waiting period for accidents, but 14 days for illnesses. usnews.com
- Certain breeds or exotic pets some insurers exclude specific dog breeds or exotic animals.

Liability coverage (homeowners) may also exclude certain breeds entirely.

Liability Coverage for Dogs (Separate From Pet Health Insurance)

- Homeowners/renters insurance usually covers injuries your dog causes to others.

- BUT: Some policies exclude certain breeds, dogs with a bite history, or exotic pets. Claims for dog bites averaged $69,000 in 2024.

This is not pet health insurance it's third-party liability.

Typical Costs

- Average monthly premium for dogs: $81.76
- Average monthly premium for cats: $43.74 (Across all 50 states + D.C.)

Best Pet Insurance Companies (2026 Rankings)

Based on U.S. News analysis:

Company	Best For	Why
ASPCA	Overall	Customizable, covers horses, no age limit
Pets Best	Budget	Lowest premiums, fast claims
MetLife	Short accident waiting period	Accident coverage starts immediately
Spot	Multiple pets	10% multi-pet discount
Embrace	Unlimited coverage	Strong accident-and-illness

Commercial Property Insurance

What Commercial Property Insurance Is

Commercial property insurance is a core business insurance policy that pays to repair, replace, or rebuild physical assets after a covered loss. It applies to:

- Buildings your business owns or leases
- Business personal property such as equipment, tools, furniture, and inventory
- Outdoor property like signs, fences, and landscaping
- Business interruption if operations are halted due to a covered event

What Events Are Typically Covered

- Fire and smoke
- Theft and vandalism
- Wind and hail
- Burst pipes
- Explosion

Important: Flood and earthquake are not included unless purchased separately.

What Types of Policies Exist

- Named-perils policy covers only listed events
- All-risk policy covers everything except exclusions
- Business Owners Policy (BOP) bundles property + liability + business interruption

Who Needs It

Any business with physical assets, including:

- Retail stores
- Offices
- Warehouses
- Restaurants
- Churches and nonprofits (if they insure buildings or equipment)

Quick Reference Table

Coverage Type	What It Protects	Best For
Building	Structure, fixtures	Owners or long-term tenants
Business personal property	Equipment, inventory	Any business with assets
Business interruption	Lost income	Businesses relying on operations
Equipment breakdown	Mechanical/electrical failure	Restaurants, manufacturers
Inland marine	Goods in transit	Contractors, delivery services

Commercial Auto Insurance

Commercial auto insurance in the United States covers vehicles used for business purposes, such as company cars, vans, trucks, and any personal vehicle used regularly for work. It protects your business from accidents, injuries, property damage, and legal liability when a vehicle is operated for business activities.

What Commercial Auto Insurance Covers

- Liability coverage Pays for injuries or property damage you cause while driving for business.
- Collision coverage Repairs your vehicle after an accident.
- Comprehensive coverage Covers theft, vandalism, weather damage, and non-collision losses.
- Medical payments Covers medical bills for you or employees after an accident.
- Uninsured/underinsured motorist Protects you if the other driver has little or no insurance. These protections apply whether you operate one vehicle or an entire fleet.

Vehicles That Typically Require Commercial Auto Insurance

- Company cars used by employees
- Pickup trucks hauling tools or equipment
- Cargo vans for deliveries or service calls
- Box trucks for moving goods
- Fleet vehicles used by multiple employees

If a vehicle is titled to a business, used to transport goods, or used for client services, insurers classify it as commercial.

Why Businesses Need It?

Commercial auto insurance protects against:

- High-cost lawsuits after accidents
- Damage to business vehicles
- Injuries to employees or third parties
- Losses from theft or vandalism

Without it, a single accident could create major financial exposure for your business.

Leading Commercial Auto Insurers (2026)

Insurer	Strength	Best For
Progressive Commercial	Strong coverage depth	Most businesses; fleets
GEICO	Affordable rates	Small businesses
The Hartford	Excellent service	Professional firms

Homeowners Insurance

Homeowners insurance is financial protection for your house, your belongings, and your liability if someone is hurt on your property. It is usually required by mortgage lenders, and it is one of the core insurance types every homeowner should understand.

What homeowners insurance actually covers

Each policy is divided into several coverage sections, not one blanket protection.

- Dwelling coverage Repairs or rebuilds your home after covered damage (fire, wind, snow, etc.). NerdWallet
- Other structures Sheds, fences, detached garages.
- Personal property Furniture, clothing, electronics if damaged or stolen.
- Liability protection If you injure someone or damage their property.
- Loss of use Pays for hotel or rental if your home becomes unlivable after a covered loss.
- Medical payments Small medical bills for guests injured on your property.

What homeowners insurance usually covers

According to NerdWallet's 2026 guide, standard policies cover:

- Fire
- Windstorms
- Snow/ice damage
- Theft
- Vandalism

What homeowners insurance does NOT cover

This is where many people get caught off guard:

- Floods requires separate flood insurance.
- Earthquakes separate policy or endorsement.
- Maintenance issues mold, rot, wear-and-tear.
- Pest damage termites, rodents.

These exclusions are emphasized across multiple insurance sources.

Why it matters

Your home is often your largest asset, and replacing it out of pocket after a disaster is impossible for most families. Homeowners insurance protects both you and your mortgage lender from catastrophic loss.

A non-obvious insight

Many people assume homeowners insurance is "one big policy," but it's actually multiple mini-policies bundled together, each with its own limits and rules. When something happens, several sections may apply at once, depending on the situation.

Understanding these sections helps you avoid under-insuring your home or being surprised during a claim.

Renters Insurance

Renters insurance protects your stuff, your liability, and your ability to live somewhere else if your rental becomes uninhabitable. That's the core idea. Everything else is details and limits.

Below is a clear, structured breakdown of what renters insurance covers, based on the most authoritative sources from Progressive and GEICO.

What Renters Insurance Covers (the essentials)

1. *Personal Property Coverage*

Protects your belongings clothes, furniture, electronics, tools, appliances if they're stolen, damaged, or destroyed by a covered event.

Examples of covered events include:

- Fire or smoke
- Theft or vandalism
- Burst pipes (water damage)
- Certain storms, wind, hail

Progressive notes this includes repair or replacement of items like clothing, electronics, furniture, tools, and appliances when damaged by a covered loss.

GEICO confirms coverage for fire, smoke, theft, vandalism, storms, and water damage from burst pipes.

2. *Personal Liability Coverage*

If someone is injured in your rental and you're legally responsible, renters insurance may pay for:

- Medical bills
- Lost wages
- Legal fees
- Property damage you cause to others

Progressive states liability may cover medical expenses, lost wages, and legal fees. progressive.com GEICO confirms liability covers injuries to visitors and legal costs.

3. Loss of Use (Temporary Living Expenses)

If your rental becomes uninhabitable due to a covered event (like a fire), renters insurance may pay for:

- Hotel stays
- Extra food costs
- Other temporary living expenses

Progressive notes this covers hotel stays and grocery expenses above normal costs. progressive.com

4. Medical Payments to Others

Covers minor injuries to guests in your home regardless of fault. This is separate from liability and usually has smaller limits.

Progressive confirms this pays for someone else's injuries even if you're not at fault.

What Renters Insurance Does NOT Cover

1. Flooding (from outside water)

Standard renters insurance does NOT cover flood damage. You need separate flood insurance for that.

Both Progressive and GEICO explicitly state flooding is not covered.

2. Earthquakes (usually)

Most policies exclude earthquakes unless you buy an add-on.

3. Damage to the building itself

Your landlord's insurance covers the structure. Your policy covers your belongings only.

4. Pet damage to your own property

If your pet destroys your carpet or walls, that's on you.

But if your pet damages someone else's property, liability may cover it. Progressive confirms this distinction.

Special Limits (Sub-Limits)

Some categories have caps, even if your total coverage is high. Common sub-limits include:

- Jewelry
- Computers
- Tools
- Cash

Progressive notes computers may have a $2,500 sub-limit and tools $1,000 unless you add a rider. If you have expensive jewelry, GEICO recommends separate jewelry insurance.

Cost of Renters Insurance

Renters insurance is cheap often $12–$15 per month.

- Progressive: "less than $1/day."
- GEICO: "as little as $12 per month."

In Florida, the average is $152/year (~$13/month).

Florida-Specific Notes (important for you in Fort Myers)

Florida renters face unique risks:

Windstorms & Hurricanes

- Wind damage is usually covered.
- But in high-risk areas, wind coverage may be separate.
- Flooding from storm surge
    - Not covered by standard renters insurance. Requires flood insurance.
- Sinkholes
    - Florida law requires coverage for catastrophic ground cover collapse, but only if the building is condemned.

Quick Summary (the simplest way to remember)

Renters insurance covers:

- Your stuff (fire, theft, storms, burst pipes)
- Your liability (injuries, property damage you cause)
- Your temporary housing (hotel if your place becomes unlivable)
- Guest medical bills

It does cover

- Flooding
- Earthquakes
- Damage to the building
- Pet damage to your own property
- High-value items beyond sub-limits unless you add riders

Condo Insurance

Condo insurance is an HO-6 policy that protects the inside of your unit and your personal belongings, filling the gaps left by your condo association's master policy. The master policy usually covers the building exterior and common areas, while you insure everything "walls-in."

Below is a clear, structured guide based on the most recent information from insurers and condo-insurance providers.

What condo insurance actually covers (HO-6)

- Interior structure walls, ceilings, flooring, cabinets, built-ins, and any upgrades you've made. (HOA master policies vary; some cover "bare walls," others "walls-in.")
- Personal property furniture, clothing, electronics, appliances, décor.
- Liability if someone is injured in your unit or you accidentally damage someone else's property.
- Loss of use hotel, meals, and living expenses if your unit becomes uninhabitable.
- Loss assessment helps pay your share of HOA-charged special assessments after a covered loss.
- Medical payments small medical bills for guests injured in your unit.

What condo insurance does NOT cover

According to Florida-area insurers, standard HO-6 policies exclude:

- Flood (must be purchased separately through NFIP)
- Earth movement
- Wear and tear / deterioration
- Pests (rodents, insects)
- Mold (limited coverage only)
- Power failure
- Intentional damage

Typical condo insurance cost

- National averages can be as low as $35/month depending on coverage and location. geico.com
- Florida coastal areas (like Fort Myers) tend to be higher due to hurricane risk.

Your rate depends on:

- Value of your belongings
- Interior upgrades
- HOA master policy type
- Deductible
- Security features (alarms, sprinklers, etc.)

What your HOA master policy covers

Every condo association is different, but typically:

- Building exterior
- Roof
- Hallways, elevators, pools, clubhouse
- Liability for common areas

Your job is to insure everything the master policy does NOT cover.

This is why reviewing your HOA's "walls-in vs. bare-walls" language is essential.

How much coverage you actually need

Use this checklist:

1. *Interior structure coverage*

Estimate the cost to replace:

- Flooring
- Cabinets
- Countertops
- Interior walls
- Fixtures
- Any upgrades (granite, tile, custom closets)

2. Personal property coverage

Walk through your unit and list:

- Furniture
- Electronics
- Clothing
- Appliances
- Décor
- Tools
- Kitchenware

(Insurers recommend a full home inventory.)

3. Liability coverage

Most owners choose $300k–$500k; higher if you have assets to protect.

4. Loss assessment

Florida condo owners often choose $5k–$50k because HOAs frequently issue special assessments after storms.

Optional add-ons worth considering

- Water backup (very common claim)
- Replacement cost for personal property (instead of actual cash value)
- Jewelry/collectibles riders
- Umbrella policy for extra liability protection (often $1M increments)

A non-obvious insight

The biggest mistake condo owners make is assuming the HOA covers more than it actually does.

Most underinsurance happens because people don't read the master policy especially in Florida, where hurricane deductibles and "walls-in" definitions vary widely.

Mobile Home Insurance

Mobile Home Insurance in the United States The Essentials

Mobile home insurance (manufactured home insurance) is a specialized policy designed for factory-built homes placed on a permanent or semi-permanent foundation. It protects the structure, your belongings, and your liability, similar to homeowners insurance but tailored to the unique risks of manufactured housing.

What a U.S. Mobile Home Policy Typically Covers

Each insurer names coverages differently, but most policies include:

- Dwelling coverage repairs or replaces the structure after covered damage.
- Personal property furniture, clothing, electronics, etc.
- Liability protection if someone is injured on your property.
- Additional living expenses hotel/meals if your home becomes unlivable.
- Wind/hail coverage included in many states, optional or separate in high-risk coastal areas.
- Flood insurance not included; must be purchased separately through NFIP or private carriers.

What Mobile Home Insurance Costs Nationally

Across the U.S., the average annual premium ranges from $700 to $1,500 depending on location, home age, and coverage limits.

Other national cost insights:

- Many sources place the average U.S. cost around $1,000–$1,300/year.
- Costs rise with older homes, higher crime areas, or severe-weather regions.
- Newer manufactured homes (post-1976 HUD code) often qualify for lower rates.

Why Costs Vary So Much by State

Mobile homes face unique risks compared to site-built homes especially wind vulnerability and transportation damage.

States with higher premiums

- Coastal states with hurricanes (FL, TX, LA, NC, SC)
- Tornado-prone states (OK, KS, AL, MS)
- States with high wildfire risk (CA)

States with lower premiums

- Northern interior states with fewer severe storms (MN, WI, MI, PA)
- Mountain states with lower population density (ID, MT, WY)

What Makes Mobile Home Insurance Different From Homeowners Insurance

Mobile homes require specialized policies because of:

- Different construction standards
- Higher wind vulnerability
- Unique anchoring/tie-down requirements
- Different replacement-cost calculations
- Exposure during transport (if newly delivered)

These distinctions are why a standard HO3 homeowners policy cannot be used for a manufactured home.

Typical Policy Components (Nationwide)

Coverage Type	What It Protects	Why It Matters
Dwelling	Structure of the home	Storms, fire, hail, wind
Personal property	Belongings	Theft, fire, storm damage
Liability	Injuries to others	Lawsuit protection
Wind/hail	Windstorm damage	Major risk in many states
Flood	Rising water	Not included in standard policies

A Non-Obvious Insight

Many U.S. mobile home owners overpay because they don't shop separately for:

- Base policy (fire, theft, liability)
- Wind/hail coverage (sometimes cheaper from a specialty carrier)
- Flood insurance (NFIP or private)

In some states, splitting these coverages can reduce premiums significantly especially in high-risk wind zones.

Earthquake Insurance

Earthquake insurance is separate coverage that protects you from damage caused by earth movement damage that regular homeowners, renters, and condo insurance does not cover.

What Earthquake Insurance Is

Earthquake insurance is a stand-alone policy or an endorsement added to your homeowners/renters/ condo policy that pays for damage caused directly by an earthquake. Standard policies exclude this under the "earth movement" exclusion.

What It Typically Covers

- Dwelling coverage Repairs to your home's structure, including foundation, walls, and roof.
- Personal property Furniture, electronics, clothing, and other belongings damaged by the quake.
- Additional living expenses Hotel stays, temporary rentals, food, and other costs if your home becomes uninhabitable.

What It Does Not Cover

- Flooding or tsunami damage (requires separate flood insurance)
- Land damage Sinkholes, land cracks, or loss of land value
- Pre-existing structural issues
- Fire following an earthquake Usually covered by standard homeowners insurance, not the earthquake policy
- Vehicle damage Covered by auto insurance with comprehensive coverage

These exclusions vary by insurer, but they are common across most policies.

Deductibles: The Big Catch

Earthquake insurance has very high deductibles, usually 5%–25% of your dwelling coverage limit. Example: If your home is insured for $400,000 and you have a 10% deductible, you must pay $40,000 out of pocket before insurance pays anything.

This is why many homeowners hesitate it's real protection, but expensive to use.

Do You Need It?

You should consider earthquake insurance if you live in or near a seismic zone. According to the U.S. Geological Survey, almost three-quarters of Americans are at risk for earthquake damage.

Florida (your location) is not a high-risk state, but earthquakes can still be felt from distant faults. Most Floridians do not buy earthquake insurance, but if you want maximum protection, it's available.

How to Decide

Use this quick guide:

Factor	Why It Matters	What to Consider
Your location risk	Higher risk = higher need	Check local seismic maps
Home type	Older homes & masonry crack easily	Frame homes fare better
Financial cushion	Can you afford repairs?	Deductibles are huge
Rebuild cost	Higher value = higher deductible	Check your dwelling limit

Bottom Line

Earthquake insurance fills a major gap in standard homeowners coverage, but it comes with high deductibles and many exclusions. It's most valuable in high-risk states (CA, WA, OR, AK), but optional in low-risk states like Florida.

Hurricane Insurance

What "Hurricane Insurance" Actually Means

There is no single hurricane insurance policy. Instead, you combine:

- Homeowners insurance covers wind, roof damage, debris, broken windows
- Flood insurance covers storm surge, rising water, flooding
- Windstorm insurance (in some states) covers wind if your homeowners policy excludes it

Together, these form what people casually call hurricane insurance.

1. *Homeowners Insurance (Wind Damage)*

Homeowners insurance covers damage caused by wind, which is a major part of hurricanes.

What it covers

- Roof damage from high winds
- Broken windows
- Exterior damage from flying debris
- Interior damage caused after wind creates an opening
- Detached structures (sheds, fences)
- Personal belongings damaged by wind-driven rain

What it does NOT cover

- Flooding
- Storm surge
- Water entering without wind-created damage

Special rule: Hurricane/Wind Deductible

Instead of a flat $500 or $1,000 deductible, hurricane-prone states use a percentage deductible:

- Typically 2%–5% of your dwelling coverage
- On a $300,000 home → $6,000–$15,000 out of pocket

This is one of the biggest surprises for homeowners.

2. *Flood Insurance (Storm Surge & Rising Water)*

Flood insurance is mandatory for full hurricane protection because homeowners insurance never covers flood.

What it covers

- Storm surge (the #1 cause of hurricane destruction)
- Rising water from heavy rain
- Flooded floors, walls, and electrical systems
- Foundation damage
- Mold (if caused by flood and mitigated promptly)
- Personal belongings (up to policy limits)

What it does NOT cover

- Temporary housing
- Swimming pools, decks, landscaping
- Cars (covered by auto insurance if you have comprehensive)

Important rule: 30-day waiting period

NFIP flood policies require a 30-day wait before coverage begins.

3. *Windstorm Insurance (Only in Certain States)*

Some coastal states exclude wind damage from standard homeowners policies.

If so, you must buy a separate windstorm policy.

What it covers

- All wind-related structural damage
- Debris damage
- Roof loss
- Wind-driven rain (if wind creates an opening)

What it doesn't cover

- Flood
- Storm surge
- Water entering without wind damage

4. *What Hurricane Insurance Costs*

Costs vary by state, but in hurricane-prone areas:

- $2,500–$8,000 per year for full hurricane protection (homeowners + flood + windstorm)

Factors affecting price:

- Distance to coast
- Elevation
- Roof type
- Age of home
- Wind-mitigation features (shutters, straps, impact windows)

5. *What Hurricane Insurance Does Not Cover (Common Surprises)*

These exclusions catch many people off guard:

- Storm surge (unless you have flood insurance)
- Water entering through closed windows
- Mold from delayed cleanup
- Loss of use (only covered if homeowners policy includes it)
- Cars (must be covered by auto comprehensive)
- Business losses (need separate business interruption coverage)

6. *Florida-Specific Notes (Important for You in Fort Myers)*

Florida has unique rules:

- Homeowners covers wind, but never flood
- Wind deductibles are 2–5% of dwelling coverage
- Flood insurance has a 30-day wait
- Florida has a 74% chance of a named storm within 50 miles in 2026

Summary: The Simple Version

To be fully protected in a hurricane, you need:

1. *Homeowners insurance → wind*
2. *Flood insurance → storm surge & rising water*
3. *Windstorm policy (if your homeowners excludes wind)*

Everything else is optional.

Umbrella Insurance

Umbrella insurance in the United States is a supplemental liability policy that adds an extra layer of protection usually in the millions on top of your auto, homeowners, or renters insurance. It exists to protect your assets and future earnings from large lawsuits that exceed your standard policy limits.

What Umbrella Insurance Is

Umbrella insurance is an optional personal liability policy that kicks in after your underlying policies (auto, home, renters, boat) reach their payout limits. It is designed for catastrophic events major accidents, lawsuits, or claims where damages can easily exceed $300,000–$500,000.

Typical coverage amounts:

- $1 million to $5 million (most common)
- Higher limits available for high-net-worth households

Cost range:

- $250–$550 per year for the first $1 million
- $75–$150 per year for each additional $1 million

What Umbrella Insurance Covers

Each item below begins with a Guided Link so you can explore any part in more depth.

- Excess liability coverage Pays when your auto/home liability limits are exhausted.
- Bodily injury liability Covers injuries you cause in accidents (e.g., multi-car crashes).
- Property damage liability Covers damage to others' property beyond your auto/home limits.
- Personal injury claims Libel, slander, defamation, false arrest, invasion of privacy. ***Coverage Advisor***
- Legal defense costs Attorney fees, court costs, settlements (often unlimited defense).
- Worldwide coverage Applies even outside the U.S. (varies by insurer).

What Umbrella Insurance Does NOT Cover

- Your own injuries or property damage
- Business-related liability (requires commercial umbrella)
- Intentional acts
- Damage to your own home or car
- Professional malpractice

Who Needs Umbrella Insurance Most

Umbrella insurance is especially recommended for people with higher liability exposure. According to ***Coverage Advisor***, the highest-risk groups include:

- Homeowners
- Landlords
- Families with teen drivers
- Dog owners
- Pool or trampoline owners
- Boat owners
- Higher-income households with assets or future earnings to protect

If you own a home in Florida, especially in a coastal city like Fort Myers, umbrella coverage is even more valuable because:

- Auto accidents with high medical costs are common.
- Lawsuits involving property, visitors, or contractors are frequent.
- Homeowners often have significant assets to protect.

How Umbrella Insurance Works (Simple Example)

1. *You cause a car accident. Damages total $1.3 million.*
2. *Your auto policy pays its limit: $300,000.*
3. *Your umbrella policy pays the remaining $1,000,000.*
4. *You pay only your underlying deductible (not the umbrella limit).*

How Much Umbrella Coverage Should You Buy?

A common rule of thumb:

Buy enough to cover your net worth + 5–10 years of future income. For many households, that means:

- $1M if you rent and have modest assets
- $2M–$3M if you own a home and have savings
- $5M+ if you have high income, rental properties, or significant assets

Cyber Liability Insurance

Cyber liability insurance in the United States protects businesses from the financial consequences of data breaches, hacking, ransomware, and other cyberattacks. It applies when your systems, data, or third-party information are compromised through digital intrusion.

What Cyber Liability Insurance Covers

- Data breaches theft or exposure of personal information such as names, SSNs, medical data, or financial records. Federal Trad...
- Hacking incidents unauthorized access to your network, servers, or cloud systems.
- Ransomware attacks extortion payments, negotiation services, and system restoration.
- Business interruption lost income when your operations shut down due to a cyberattack.
- Vendor/third-party cyber incidents attacks on data stored with outside providers.
- Worldwide cyber events coverage applies even if the attack originates outside the United States.
- Regulatory defense legal defense for investigations after a breach.
- Third-party liability claims from customers, clients, or partners harmed by your breach.

First-Party vs. Third-Party Coverage

Coverage Type	What It Protects
First-party	Your own losses: data recovery, ransomware payments, business interruption
Third-party	Claims against you: lawsuits, regulatory fines, customer damages

Key Cyber Events That Trigger Coverage

- Hacking unauthorized access to systems or accounts.
- Phishing/BEC fraudulent emails leading to data theft or financial loss.
- Malware infections viruses, trojans, or spyware damaging systems.
- Ransomware encryption of data with extortion demands.
- Data theft stolen customer or employee information.

Business Interruption Insurance

Business interruption insurance covers lost income after a disaster, but only when the disaster causes direct physical damage to your property and is a covered peril. That's the key condition.

Business interruption insurance is specifically designed to replace the income your business would have earned if the disaster had not occurred. It also pays ongoing expenses like payroll, rent, taxes, and loan payments during the shutdown period.

What It Does Cover (When Triggered)

- Lost income/profits based on your historical financial records.
- Operating expenses that continue even while closed (rent, payroll, taxes, loan payments).
- Extra expenses to speed reopening (temporary location, equipment rental, overtime labor).
- Civil authority shutdowns (e.g., mandatory evacuation) if caused by nearby physical damage.

What It Does NOT Cover

- Flood or earthquake damage these require separate flood or earthquake policies.
- Pandemics or virus-related closures (COVID-type events).
- Government shutdowns not tied to physical damage. *compare.com*
- Utility outages off your property unless you bought a special endorsement.

The Triggering Rule (Most Important Part)

Coverage begins only if:

1. *A covered peril (fire, hurricane wind, explosion, etc.)*
2. *Causes direct physical damage to your insured property*
3. *And that damage forces you to suspend operations*

Without physical damage, the policy does not activate.

Bottom Line

Business interruption insurance replaces lost income after disasters, but only when the disaster causes covered physical damage.

If the damage is excluded (like flood), the lost income is also excluded.

Workers' Compensation Insurance

Workers' compensation insurance

What workers' comp covers

- Medical treatment doctor visits, hospital care, surgery, prescriptions, physical therapy.
- Lost wages partial wage replacement (usually 2/3 of average weekly wage).
- Disability benefits temporary or permanent, partial or total.
- Rehabilitation vocational retraining if the worker cannot return to their prior job.
- Death benefits payments to dependents + funeral expenses.

What workers' comp does NOT cover

This is the part this book will emphasize the exclusions people rarely understand.

- Injuries outside the scope of employment commuting, lunch breaks off-premises, personal errands.
- Self-inflicted injuries including fights the employee starts.
- Intoxication or drug-related injuries if impairment caused the accident.
- Horseplay or rule violations injuries from reckless behavior.
- Independent contractors unless misclassified.
- Off-the-clock activities unless employer benefits directly.

Florida-specific requirements (Fort Myers applies these rules)

Florida is strict:

- Construction employers must carry coverage with 1+ employees, including owners.
- Non-construction employers — must carry coverage with 4+ employees.
- Agricultural employers 6+ regular employees or 12+ seasonal.
- Out-of-state contractors must carry Florida-compliant coverage while working in the state.

Who is covered?

- Employees performing job duties.
- Corporate officers (may exempt themselves depending on industry).
- Some contractors if they meet the legal definition of "employee."

Long-Term Care

Long-term care breaks into four major categories each with different levels of support, cost, and insurance coverage. Below is a clear, structured guide so you can compare nursing homes, assisted living, in home care, and long-term care insurance, with citations from the most recent 2025–2026 data.

The four pillars of long-term care

In-Home Care

In home care provides one on one help at home, ranging from basic personal care to skilled nursing.

- Supports independence; ideal when someone wants to "age in place."
- Services include bathing, dressing, medication help, wound care, and therapy.
- Home health care is appropriate when medical needs are moderate and safety can be maintained at home.
- According to U.S. News, home health care focuses on independence with individualized services, unlike nursing homes which provide 24/7 oversight.

Typical cost: National average around $198/day for home care services.

Assisted Living

Assisted living is for people who need help with daily activities but do not require constant medical supervision.

- Provides meals, housekeeping, social activities, and personal care.
- Often includes memory care units for dementia.
- More independence than a nursing home, but more support than living at home.

Typical cost: Median monthly costs vary by state; national averages are tracked annually by A Place for Mom.

Nursing Homes

Nursing homes provide 24/7 medical care, supervision, and rehabilitation.

- Best for people with significant medical needs, mobility issues, or cognitive decline.
- Offer skilled nursing, physical therapy, occupational therapy, and speech therapy.
- Facilities like those described by Lee Health include comprehensive rehab, wound care, IV therapy, and respiratory support.

Typical cost: National average around $308/day for a nursing home.

Long-Term Care Insurance

Long-term care insurance helps pay for:

- Nursing homes
- Assisted living
- Home health aides
- Adult day care
- Memory care

It is designed to protect savings from being drained by long term care costs.

- Policies vary widely in coverage, daily benefit amounts, and inflation protection.
- Many people buy LTC insurance in their 50s–60s, before premiums rise sharply.

You can estimate future costs using long term care cost calculators that project expenses by state and care type.

What determines which option is right?

Key decision factors

- Medical needs Do you need 24/7 supervision or just help with daily tasks?
- Mobility & safety Is the home environment safe?
- Cognitive status Dementia often requires memory care or nursing home support.

- Budget Nursing homes are the most expensive; in home care varies by hours needed.
- Family support In home care works best when family can supplement care.

Cost snapshot (national averages)

Care Type	Typical Cost	Best For
In-home care	~$198/day	Independence + moderate needs
Assisted living	Varies by state; median monthly costs tracked by A Place for Mom	Help + social environment
Nursing home	~$308/day	High medical needs + 24/7 care
LTC insurance	Premiums vary	Protecting assets + planning ahead

Most families wait until a medical crisis forces a decision which experts warn against. Planning early allows you to:

- Compare facilities
- Understand insurance options
- Avoid overpaying
- Make decisions calmly rather than in an emergency

Care.com notes that families often face major financial decisions suddenly after a crisis, which leads families to rush and make incorrect choices.

Medicare: What it does and does not pay for

1. *Medicare does not pay for long term custodial care*

Custodial care includes help with bathing, dressing, eating, toileting, and supervision the core of nursing homes, assisted living, and in home personal care.

Medicare explicitly states that it doesn't pay for long term care.

2. *What Medicare does cover*

Medicare only covers short term, skilled care after a qualifying hospital stay:

- Skilled nursing facility (SNF) care
- Physical, occupational, or speech therapy
- Wound care, IV therapy, rehab
- Medical supplies and doctor services while in a facility

3. *The "100-day cliff"*

Medicare covers up to 100 days of skilled nursing facility care per benefit period and only if the patient is improving and still needs skilled services. Families often learn this around day 80 when discharge planners warn that Medicare coverage is ending.

After day 100, Medicare stops paying entirely, and the full cost shifts to the family.

4. *Medicare still matters even in a nursing home*

Even though Medicare doesn't pay for the room and board:

- It still covers hospitalizations
- Doctor visits
- Medications (Part D)
- Medical equipment
- Preventive care

Medicare notes that you can switch drug plans anytime while living in a nursing home.

Medicaid: The primary payer for long term care

1. *Medicaid does pay for long term custodial care*

Medicaid is the only major government program that pays for indefinite long term care including nursing homes, assisted living (in some states), and in home care.

2. *Medicaid is state specific*

Rules, benefits, and names vary by state. For example, Florida Medicaid pays for long term care in:

- Nursing homes

- Assisted living
- In home care through programs like:
    - Nursing Home Medicaid
    - Statewide Medicaid Managed Care Long-Term Care (SMMC LTC)
    - Medicaid for Aged and Disabled (MEDS-AD)

3. Eligibility

Medicaid requires:

- Low income and limited assets
- Functional need (must require a “nursing home level of care”)

Many middle class families eventually qualify through spend down, Medicaid planning, or spousal protection rules.

4. *What Medicaid covers*

Depending on the state:

- Nursing home room and board (fully covered once eligible)
- Assisted living (often partially covered through waivers)
- In home personal care
- Adult day care
- Memory care
- Medical transportation
- Case management

5. *Why Medicaid becomes essential*

With nursing homes averaging $10,000 per month in 2026, most families cannot pay privately for long.

The non-obvious truth

Most families assume Medicare will pay for nursing homes and are shocked when it doesn’t. The financial burden hits suddenly after Medicare’s 100-day limit, forcing families to pay out of pocket until Medicaid eligibility is reached.

Vision Insurance

What is Vision Insurance

Vision insurance is a cost-sharing plan that reduces what you pay for routine eye care. You pay a monthly premium, and in return you receive allowances, copays, and discounts for eye exams and eyewear.

It is not major medical insurance. It does not cover eye diseases or medical eye problems those fall under regular health insurance.

What Vision Insurance Typically Covers

Each plan varies, but most include:

- Routine eye exams usually once every 12 months with a small copay (often $10–$20). Source: UnitedHealthcare notes that vision plans cover routine exams from day one. uhc.com
- Prescription eyeglasses coverage usually includes:•
- Standard lenses (single-vision, bifocal, trifocal)
- A frame allowance (commonly $120–$200)
- Discounts on upgrades (anti-glare, progressive lenses)
- Contact lenses either instead of glasses or as a separate allowance. Most plans cover both glasses and contacts, depending on the state.
- Lens enhancements partial coverage or discounts for coatings, transitions, high-index lenses.
- LASIK discounts not full coverage, but many plans offer 10–20% off. EyeMed specifically advertises LASIK savings.

What Vision Insurance Does Not Cover

Vision insurance is not designed for medical eye care. These are covered by your health insurance instead:

- Eye infections
- Cataracts
- Glaucoma
- Diabetic eye disease
- Emergency eye injuries
- Medically necessary surgeries

Vision insurance is strictly for routine care and corrective eyewear.

How Vision Insurance Works

Vision insurance uses a simple structure:

1. *Premium*

You pay a monthly fee (often $10–$25 for individuals).

2. *Copays*

A small fixed amount for services (e.g., $10 for an exam).

3. *Allowances*

A set dollar amount toward frames or contacts (e.g., $150 frame allowance).

4. *Network Providers*

You save the most when using in-network optometrists and optical retailers. VSP and UnitedHealthcare both emphasize large national networks.

5. *Frequency Limits*

Most plans allow:

- One exam every 12 months
- One pair of glasses every 12–24 months
- Contacts once per year (in place of glasses)

Major Vision Insurance Providers

- VSP — the largest vision insurer; strong private-practice network.
- EyeMed — large retail network (LensCrafters, Target Optical).
- UnitedHealthcare Vision — flexible plans, no waiting periods.

Why People Buy Vision Insurance

Vision insurance is usually worth it if:

- You wear glasses or contacts every year
- You want predictable costs for exams and eyewear
- You prefer brand-name frames (which can be expensive without coverage)
- You have children (kids' prescriptions change often)

It may be less necessary if you have perfect vision and rarely need exams.

Typical Cost Savings

A routine eye exam alone can cost $80–$150 without insurance. Glasses can range $150–$400+ depending on frames and lenses.

A vision plan costing $15/month ($180/year) often pays for itself with:

- One exam
- One pair of glasses or contacts
- Lens enhancements discounts

Quick Comparison Table

Feature	VSP	EyeMed	UnitedHealthcare Vision
Network	Large private-practice focus	Strong retail network	Large national network
Exam Copay	Typically $10–$20	Typically $10	Typically $10
Frame Allowance	$150–$200 typical	$130–$200 typical	Varies by plan
Contacts	Annual allowance	Annual allowance	Annual allowance
LASIK	Discounts	Discounts	Discounts
Waiting Period	None	None	None

Dental Insurance

What Dental Insurance Covers (The 3-Tier System)

Most plans divide dental care into three categories, each with different coverage levels.

1. *Preventive Care*

Usually covered at 100% with no deductible and no waiting period. Includes:

- Cleanings (typically 2 per year)
- Routine exams
- X-rays
- Fluoride for children

Insurers emphasize preventive care because it reduces expensive problems later. uhc.com

2. *Basic Services*

Typically covered at 50–80% after deductible. Includes:

- Fillings
- Simple extractions
- Emergency treatment for dental pain

Many plans have a waiting period (often 3–6 months) before these benefits begin.

3. *Major Services*

Usually covered at 30–50% after deductible, with a longer waiting period (6–12 months). Includes:

- Crowns
- Root canals
- Bridges
- Dentures
- Implants (only on some plans)

Coverage varies widely some low-cost plans exclude implants entirely.

How Dental Insurance Works Financially

Dental insurance has several cost components:

- Premium

Your monthly payment for the plan.

- Deductible

What you pay out-of-pocket before insurance starts paying for basic/major services.

- Coinsurance

Your share of the cost after the deductible (e.g., 20% of a filling).

Example from UnitedHealthcare: a $100 filling with 30% coinsurance means you pay $30.

- Copay

A fixed fee for certain services (more common in HMO plans).

- Annual Maximum

Most plans cap how much they will pay per year often $1,000–$2,000. Once you hit the cap, you pay 100% of additional costs.

Types of Dental Plans

1. *PPO Plans (Most Common)*

- Large dentist network
- You can go out-of-network (but pay more)
- Preventive care often free
- Deductible + coinsurance apply
- Annual maximum applies

PPOs dominate the U.S. market.

2. *HMO / DHMO Plans*

- Lower premiums
- Must choose a primary dentist
- No out-of-network coverage
- Often no deductible or annual maximum
- Fixed copays for procedures

3. *Dental Discount Plans (Not insurance)*

- Pay a membership fee
- Receive discounted rates from participating dentists
- No waiting periods
- No annual maximum

These are alternatives when traditional insurance is too expensive.

Orthodontics (Braces & Aligners)

Coverage varies widely:

- Many adult plans do not cover orthodontics
- Many family plans cover children only
- When covered, orthodontics often has a separate lifetime maximum (e.g., $1,000–$2,000)

What Dental Insurance Usually Does Not Cover

- Cosmetic procedures (whitening, veneers)
- Adult orthodontics (unless a premium plan)
- Implants (excluded on many basic plans)
- TMJ treatment (varies)
- Orthognathic surgery (often medical, not dental)

Each insurer has its own exclusions.

Why Dental Insurance Matters

Major insurers emphasize three benefits:

- People with dental insurance are more likely to get preventive care.
- Preventive care reduces expensive procedures later.
- Oral health is linked to overall health (heart disease, diabetes).

Dear Reader,

Thank you for walking with me through this complicated, often frustrating world of insurance. I know it isn't simple, and it isn't always fair, but you stayed with it page after page determined to understand what so many people never take the time to learn. That alone puts you ahead of the maze.

My hope is that this book has given you more than information. I hope it has given you clarity, confidence, and the ability to see through the fog that insurance companies often create. Most of all, I hope it has shown you not just what's included, but what's not the part that truly protects you.

If even one chapter helped you avoid a surprise, ask a better question, or stand up for yourself when something didn't feel right, then this work has done its job. You deserve to feel informed, prepared, and empowered, not confused or intimidated.

Thank you for trusting me to guide you. May this book continue to serve as your map, your compass, and your steady light as you navigate the maze of insurance today, tomorrow, and every time life asks you to make a decision that truly matters.

Author
Andrew De Carlo